Celebrating Special Days

Worship Services for All Occasions

Abingdon Press

CELEBRATING SPECIAL DAYS

Copyright © 1997 by Abingdon Press

ISBN 0-687-05278-5

01 02 03 04 05 06 — 10 9 8 7 6 5 4 3

MANUFACTURED IN THE UNITED STATES OF AMERICA

Contents

The Advent Wreath

FIRST SUNDAY—ANTICIPATION

LEADER: "Take heed, watch; for you do not know when the time will come" (Mark 13:33).

PEOPLE: **We watch and wait in anticipation for the coming of the Christ Child. We prepare our hearts and minds for his coming. We submit our lives to the transforming power of his continued return.**

LEADER: The first candle in the Advent wreath represents our anticipation, both this year and in years gone by.

PRAYER: **Dear God, as we light the first candle in our Advent wreath, we confess our lack of eagerness, our unwillingness to become excited about Christmas. We pray that you will change our dull selves into exciting, vibrant children of God, that you will make watching and waiting in anticipation our bywords. Amen.**

SECOND SUNDAY—PREPARATION

LEADER: "In the wilderness prepare the way of the LORD, make straight in the desert a highway for our God" (Isa. 40:3).

PEOPLE: **As we wait in darkness, our hope is rekindled by the light of the Lord shining in the night. We offer our lives to serve the Lord with our renewed hope.**

LEADER: Last week we lit the first candle in our Advent wreath-the candle of anticipation.

(Light one purple candle in the Advent wreath.)

LEADER: Today we come to the wreath again, our anticipation a part of our lives. We light the second candle, the candle of preparation, for we would learn to be straighteners and builders of a highway of God.

PRAYER: **We confess that while sometimes we do become excited with our anticipation of Christmas, we display a lack of preparation when the day finally arrives. Help us overcome** the frenzy and disorganization of our Advent celebration. Send us the gift of preparation to balance our sense of anticipation. Amen.

THIRD SUNDAY—WAITING

LEADER: "Rejoice always, pray constantly, give thanks in all circumstances; for this is the will of God in Christ Jesus for you" (1 Thess. 5:16-18).

PEOPLE: **As the light begins to push away the corners of darkness, as the time grows closer, we find ourselves needing more patience. We give ourselves to you to help us in our waiting.**

LEADER: Last week we lit the second Advent candle, the candle of preparation. Before that, we lit the first candle, the candle of anticipation.

(Light two purple candles in the Advent wreath.)

LEADER: Now we light the third Advent candle as we gather around our wreath in patient waiting, for we would be prepared, excited, and yet patient!

(Light the third purple candle or the pink candle.)

PRAYER: **We confess that we often are unable to wait, and hence our lives are marked by hurry and anxiety. We pray for patience— a patience that will transform our lives so that we may live with Christmas peace the whole year through. Amen.**

FOURTH SUNDAY—ANNUNCIATION

LEADER: "He will be great, and will be called the Son of the Most High; and the Lord God will give to him the throne of his father David, and he will reign over the house of Jacob for ever" (Luke 1:32-33a).

PEOPLE: **As the angel voices announce the coming of the Son of God, so we hear God's promises, and we surrender ourselves to God's direction.**

LEADER: Last week we lit the third candle, the candle of waiting. Before that, we lit the candle of anticipation and the candle of preparation.

(Light two purple candles and the pink candle, or three purple candles.)

LEADER: Today we light the fourth candle, the candle of annunciation. We hear angel voices telling us of the coming of the Christ Child, just as shepherds did years ago.

(Light the last purple candle.)

PRAYER: **So often we are unable to hear God's word for us because we are occupied with other things. Sometimes we do not hear because of the level of noise we create for ourselves. We pray for silence on our part, so we can hear your words for us today and obey. Amen.**

CHRISTMAS—FULFILLMENT

LEADER: Glory to God in the highest, and on earth peace! (Luke 2:14).

PEOPLE: **Today we experience the fulfillment of our anticipation, our waiting. Just as Jesus enters the world, we welcome him to enter our lives.**

LEADER: We have lighted the candles of anticipation, preparation, waiting, and annunciation.

(Light all candles except the Christ [white] candle.)

LEADER: Now we gather around the wreath to light the Christ candle, the candle of fulfillment.

(Light the white candle in the center of the Advent wreath.)

PRAYER: **Dear God, we confess that often the tinsel and glitter of Christmas occupy more of our thoughts and time than the Christ Child. We pray that this time of fulfillment will transform our lives; and fulfilled, that we will serve you the whole year through. Amen.**

Christ Has Come to Earth

A Christmas Candlelighting Service

PRELUDE: "Once in Royal David's City"

CALL TO WORSHIP (Unison)

God so loved the world, that he gave his only begotten Son, that whosoever believeth in him should not perish, but have everlasting life. John 3:16 KJV

OPENING HYMN: "Come, Thou Long-Expected Jesus"

PRAYER:

Dear God, simply but sincerely we lift our hearts to you, saying, "Thank you for Jesus!" We remember the first announcement of his coming and the words that linger in our memories: "Fear not . . . good tidings . . . great joy . . . all people . . . Savior . . . Christ the Lord."

It is a long way from Bethlehem to our homes; it is a long way from the manger in the stable to a bed in our hearts; it is a long time from that first Christmas to this Christmas; but as new life came into the world then, it is our faith that it can come into our lives today.

Over the tumult and the noise of our world, may we hear the voice of Christ ringing clear and true, speaking the words of peace and reconciliation. Hear us now as we pray as he taught us, saying:

THE LORD'S PRAYER

THE BIRTH OF THE SAVIOR FORETOLD

SCRIPTURE: Isaiah 9:2, 6-7

CAROL: "O Come, O Come Emmanuel" (1 & 2)

SCRIPTURE: Isaiah 11:1-4a, 6-9

CAROL: "O Come, O Come Emmanuel" (3 & 4)

THE ANNUNCIATION

SCRIPTURE: Luke 1:26-35, 38

HYMN: "Come, Christians, Join to Sing"

HE IS BORN!

SCRIPTURE: Luke 2:1-7

CAROL: "O Little Town of Bethlehem"

CAROL: "Away in a Manger"

THE SHEPHERDS AND THE ANGELS

SCRIPTURE: Luke 2:8-16

CAROL: "The First Noel"

CAROL: "Infant Holy, Infant Lowly"

THE VISIT OF THE WISE MEN

SCRIPTURE: Matthew 2:1-11

CAROL: "We Three Kings"

THE LIGHT SHINES IN THE DARKNESS

SCRIPTURE: John 1:1-5

MEDITATION

OFFERING

SERVICE OF CANDLELIGHTING

(As "Silent Night" is sung, the lights will be dimmed, and the pastor will light the candles of the candlelighters gathered at the altar. They will light the candle of the first worshiper in each pew. Light will then be passed from worshiper to worshiper. Remember that the lighted candle remains upright, and the unlighted candle is tipped to be lighted.)

CAROL: "Silent Night"

BENEDICTION

PASTOR: The peace of God which passes all understanding keep your hearts and minds in the knowledge and love of God and of his Son, Jesus Christ our Lord; and the blessing of God Almighty, the Father, the Son, and the Holy Spirit, be among you and remain with you always.

PEOPLE: Amen. Thanks be to God!

A Covenant Service in the Tradition of Wesley

An order of worship for all who wish to enter into or renew their covenant with God. For use in a Watch Night service, on New Year's Eve, the first Sunday of the year, or other special occasions.

(Note: On December 26, 1747, John Wesley strongly urged the Methodists to renew their covenant with God. His first Covenant Service was held on August 11, 1755. This service follows Wesley's original closely, with occasional changes in the language.)

PRELUDE

HYMN OF PRAISE: "I'll Praise My Maker While I've Breath"

COLLECT FOR PURITY (In unison)

Almighty God, unto whom all hearts are open, all desires known, and from whom no secrets are hid; cleanse the thoughts of our hearts by the inspiration of thy Holy Spirit, that we may perfectly love thee, and worthily magnify the holy name; through Christ our Lord. Amen.

THE LORD'S PRAYER

SCRIPTURE LESSON: John 15:1-8

HYMN OF INVITATION: "Blessed Jesus at Thy Word"

THE INVITATION (The Pastor)

Dearly beloved, the Christian life, to which we are called, is a life in Christ redeemed from sin by him, and through him consecrated to God. Upon this life we have entered, having been admitted into that new covenant of which our Lord Jesus Christ is mediator, and which he sealed with his own blood, that it might stand forever.

On one side, the covenant is God's promise to fulfill in and through us, all that God declared in Jesus Christ, who is the author and perfecter of our faith. That this promise still stands we are sure, for we have known God's goodness and proved God's grace in our lives day by day.

On the other side, we stand pledged to live no more unto ourselves, but to him who loved us and gave himself for us and called us to serve him, that the purposes of his coming be fulfilled.

From time to time we renew our vows of consecration, especially when we gather at the table of the Lord; but on this day we meet expressly, as generations of our forebears have met, that we may joyfully and solemnly renew the covenant which bound them and binds us to God.

Let us then, remembering the mercies of God and the hope of God's calling, examine ourselves by the light of the Spirit, that we may see wherein we have failed or fallen short in faith and practice and, considering all that this covenant means, may give ourselves anew to God. Let us pray.

ADORATION

Let us adore the Father, the God of love who created us; who every moment preserves and sustains us; who has loved us with an everlasting love, and given us the light of the knowledge of divine glory in the face of Jesus Christ.

PEOPLE: **We praise you, O God; we acknowledge you to be the Lord.**

PASTOR: Let us glory in the grace of our Lord Jesus Christ; who, though he was rich, yet for our sakes became poor;
who went about doing good and preaching the gospel of the kingdom;
who was tempted in all ways just as we are, yet did not sin;
who became obedient unto death, even the death of a cross;
who was dead, yet lives now and forever;
who opened the kingdom of heaven to all believers;
who sits now at the right hand of God.

PEOPLE: **We praise you, O Christ. You are the King of glory.**

PASTOR: Let us rejoice in the fellowship of the Holy Spirit,
the Lord and Giver of life,
by whom we are born into the family of God,
and become members of the body of Christ;
whose witness confirms us;
whose power enables us;
who waits to do for us exceeding abundantly above all that we ask or think.

PEOPLE: **All praise to you, O Holy Spirit.**

THANKSGIVING

PASTOR: Please stand as you are able. Let us give thanks for God's manifold blessings.
O God our Father, the fountain of all goodness, you have been gracious to us all the years of our life; We give thanks to you

for your loving-kindness which has filled our days and brought us to this time and place.

PEOPLE: **We praise your holy name, O Lord.**

PASTOR: You have given us life and reason, and set us in a world which is full of your glory. You have comforted us with family and friends, and ministered to us through the hands and minds of our neighbors.

PEOPLE: **We praise your holy name, O Lord.**

PASTOR: Our hearts hunger for you, O Lord, and you have filled us with peace. You have redeemed us and called us to a high calling in Christ Jesus. You have given us a place in the fellowship of your Spirit and the witness of your church.

PEOPLE: **We praise your holy name, O Lord.**

PASTOR: You have been our light in the darkness, our strength in times of adversity and temptation, the very spirit of joy in joyful times, and the all-sufficient reward of our labors.

PEOPLE: **We praise your holy name, O Lord.**

PASTOR: You remember us when we have forgotten you, followed us even when we fled you, met us with forgiveness when we turned back to you. For all your long-suffering and the abundance of your grace,

PEOPLE: **We praise your holy name, O Lord.**

PASTOR: Be seated and join me in the prayer of confession.

Let us now examine ourselves before God, humbly confessing our sins and watching our hearts, lest by self-deceit we shut ourselves out from his presence.

O God our Father, who set forth the way of life for us in your beloved Son: We confess with shame our slowness to learn of him, our reluctance to follow him. You have called us and we have not answered. Your beauty has shone forth, but we have not seen. You have stretched out your hands to us through our neighbors, but we have passed by. We have taken much, but given little thanks; We have been unworthy of your changeless love.

PEOPLE:	**Have mercy on us, and forgive us, O Lord.**
PASTOR:	Forgive us for the poverty of our worship, the formality and selfishness of our prayers, our inconstancy and unbelief, our neglect of fellowship and of the means of grace, our hesitating witness for Christ, our false pretenses, and our willful ignorance of your ways.
PEOPLE:	**Have mercy on us, and forgive us, O Lord.**
PASTOR:	Forgive us for wasting our time and misusing our gifts. Forgive us for attempting to excuse our wrongdoings and for evading our responsibilities. Forgive us for being unwilling to overcome evil with good. Forgive us for drawing back from the cross.
PEOPLE:	**Have mercy on us and forgive us, O Lord.**
PASTOR:	Forgive us for letting so little of your love reach others through us. Forgive us for overlooking the wrongs and sufferings that were not our own. Forgive us for cherishing the things that divide us from others, making it hard for them to live with us. Forgive us for being thoughtless in our judgments, hasty in condemnation, grudging in forgiveness.
PEOPLE:	**Have mercy on us and forgive us, O Lord.**
PASTOR:	If we have made no ventures in fellowship, if we have kept in our hearts a grievance against another, if we have not sought reconciliation, if we have been eager for the punishment of wrongdoers and slow to seek their redemption,
PEOPLE:	**Have mercy on us and forgive us, O Lord.**
PASTOR:	Let each of us in silence make our confession to God.

After a period of silent prayer the pastor and people shall say,

Have mercy on me, O God, according to your loving kindness; according to the multitude of your tender mercies blot out my transgressions. Wash me thoroughly from my iniquity, and cleanse me from my sin. Create in me a clean heart, O God; and renew a right spirit with me. Amen.

PASTOR:	This is the message we have heard from God, and proclaim to you: God is light and in God there is no darkness at all. If

we walk in the light, as God is in the light, we have fellowship one with another, and the blood of Jesus Christ washes away our sin. If we say we have no sin, we deceive ourselves, and the truth is not in us. If we confess our sins, God is faithful and just to forgive us our sins and to cleanse us from all unrighteousness.

COVENANT HYMN: "Come, Let Us Use the Grace Divine" or
"I Want to Walk as a Child of the Light."

THE COVENANT

PASTOR: And now, beloved, let us bind ourselves with willing bonds to our covenant God, and take the yoke of Christ upon us.

This taking of his yoke upon us means that we are heartily content that he appoints us our place and work, and he alone be our reward.

Christ has many services to be done. Some are easy, others are difficult; some bring honor, others bring reproach; some are suitable to our natural inclinations and temporal interests, others are contrary to both.

In some we may please Christ and please ourselves; in others we cannot please Christ except by denying ourselves.

Yet the power to do all these things is assuredly given us in Christ, who strengthens us.

Therefore, let us make the covenant of God our own. Let us engage our heart to the Lord, and resolve in his strength never to go back.

Being thus prepared, let us now, in sincere dependence on God's grace and trusting in God's promises, yield ourselves anew to the Lord.

Let us pray:

O Lord God, you called us through Jesus Christ to be partakers in this gracious covenant; we take upon ourselves with joy the yoke of obedience, and engage ourselves, for love of you, to seek and to do your perfect will. We are no longer our own, but yours.

ALL: **I am no longer my own, but yours. Put me to what you will, rank me with whom you will; put me to doing, put me to suffering; let me be employed for you or laid aside for you, exalted for you or brought low for you; let me be full, let me be empty; let me have all things, let me have nothing; I freely and heartily yield all things to your pleasure and disposal.**

And now, O glorious and blessed God, Father, Son, and Holy Spirit, you are mine, and I belong to you. So be it. And the covenant which I have made on earth, let it be ratified in heaven. Amen.

PASTOR: Lift up your hearts.

PEOPLE: **We lift them up to the Lord.**

PASTOR: It is not only right, but it is our duty that we should at all times and in all places give thanks to you, O Lord, holy Father, almighty, everlasting God.

Therefore with angels and archangels, and with all the company of heaven, we laud and magnify your glorious name, forever giving praise to you and saying:

ALL: **Holy, holy, holy, Lord God of hosts: Heaven and earth are full of your glory! Glory be to you, O Lord most high! Amen.**

THE APOSTLES' CREED (unison)

GLORIA PATRI

Here may follow Holy Communion, or a sermon.

THE OFFERING

PASTOR: O God, who has greatly loved us, long sought us, and mercifully redeemed us, give us grace that in everything we may yield ourselves, our wills, and our works, a continual thank offering to you through Jesus Christ our Lord. Amen.

DOXOLOGY

HYMN OF DEDICATION: "Sent Forth by God's Blessing"

BENEDICTION

One Great Hour of Sharing

GATHERING

GREETING

CALL TO WORSHIP

PASTOR: Our very lives are God's gift to us.

PEOPLE: **We come to praise God for these gifts.**

PASTOR: In this needy world of ours, we are called to be gift givers,

PEOPLE: **Offering our material possessions, our skills, our talents, and our beings.**

PASTOR: In sharing our lives, we are blessed.

PEOPLE: **In sharing our lives, we draw closer to the Kingdom.**

HYMN OF PRAISE

OLD TESTAMENT
(1 Samuel 16:1-3; II Chronicles 36:14-23; Joshua 5:9-12)

PRAYER OF CONFESSION

O God of Plenty, you desire good for all. Yet we choose to horde rather than to share. Millions starve while we diet. We confess that we gladly give our leftovers to those we deem worthy, reserving the best for ourselves. Teach us to share all we have and all we are, that your love might be seen throughout the world. In the name of Jesus, who gave his life, Amen.

WORDS OF ASSURANCE

Our God is a forgiving God who calls us from repentance to active caring. As people who have experienced forgiveness, let us open ourselves to the call of God in our lives.

RESPONSIVE READING (Psalm 23; Psalm 137:1-6; Psalm 34:1-8)

ANTHEM

EPISTLE
(Ephesians 5:8-14; Ephesians 2:4-10; II Corinthians 5:16-21)

PRAYERS OF THE PEOPLE with the Lord's Prayer

OFFERING with Doxology

HYMN OF PREPARATION

GOSPEL (John 9:1-41; John 3:14-21; Luke 15:1-3, 11-32)

Suggested: John 21:15-17

SERMON

Jesus still asks whether we love him. The obvious response is yes! But this answer requires action. Use local examples of ways Christian action is taking place: food cupboards, advocacy groups, and so on. The sermon may then move into ways people still do not receive care: the rising rate of homelessness, lack of health care, and other needs. We are mandated by our faith to be the caretakers of our world.

SPECIAL OFFERING with Prayer

O God, make us generous people, willing to give of all we have, rather than merely from our leftovers. In the name of the One who shared himself, **Amen.**

LITANY OF SHARING

PASTOR: Lord, teach us to share. Where there are empty stomachs,

PEOPLE: **Let us share food.**

PASTOR: Where there are empty hearts,

PEOPLE: **Let us share love.**

PASTOR: Where there are no beds,

PEOPLE: **Let us share our homes.**

PASTOR: Where there is no vision for the future,

PEOPLE: **Let us share hope.**

ALL: **God, we hear you ask, "Do you love me?" Teach us to respond in action. We are here to feed your sheep. Amen.**

HYMN OF DEDICATION

BENEDICTION

A Service of Tenebrae

PRELUDE "Jesus, Joy of Man's Desiring"

CALL TO WORSHIP

And this is the judgment, that the light has come into the world, and we loved darkness rather than light.

God is light, in whom there is no darkness at all.

For God sent the Son into the world, not to condemn the world, but that the world might be saved through him.

Every one who does evil hates the light, and does not come to the light. But all who do what is true come to the light.

HYMN: "O Love Divine, What Hast Thou Done"

> O Love divine, what hast thou done!
> The immortal God had died for me!
> The Father's co-eternal Son
> bore all my sins upon the tree.
> Th' immortal God for me hath died:
> My Lord, my Love, is crucified!
>
> Is crucified for me and you,
> to bring us rebels back to God.
> Believe, believe the record true,
> ye all are bought with Jesus' blood.
> Pardon for all flows from his side:
> My Lord, my Love, is crucified!
>
> Behold him, all ye that pass by,
> the bleeding Prince of life and peace!
> Come sinners, see your Savior die,
> and say, "Was ever grief like his?"
> Come, feel with me this blood applied:
> My Lord, my Love, is crucified!

OPENING PRAYER:

The Lord be with you.
And also with you.

Let us pray: (A brief silence.)

Most gracious God,
Look with mercy upon your family
gathered here for who our Lord Jesus
Christ was betrayed, given into sinful
hands, and suffered death upon the
cross.
Strengthen our faith and forgive our
betrayals as we enter the way of
his passion;
through him who lives and reigns with
you and the Holy Spirit, now and for
ever. **Amen.**

(Seven candles and the Christ candle are lit on the altar. After each of the
readings, one of the candles is extinguished. After the eighth reading, a loud
noise is heard and the Christ candle is removed, symbolizing the death of our
Lord.)

FIRST READING: Mark 14:26-42

SECOND READING: Mark 14:43-50

THIRD READING: Mark 14:51-72

FOURTH READING: Mark 15:1-5

FIFTH READING: Mark 15:6-15

HYMN: "Ah, Holy Jesus"

Ah, holy Jesus, how hast thou offended,
That we to judge thee hath in hate
pretended?
By foes derided, by thine own rejected,
O most afflicted!

Who was the guilty? Who brought this upon
    thee?
Alas, my treason, Jesus hath undone thee!
"Twas I, Lord Jesus, I it was denied thee;
I crucified thee.

For me, kind Jesus, was thy incarnation.
Thy mortal sorrow, and thy life's oblation;
Thy death of anguish and thy bitter
    passion,
For my salvation.

Therefore, kind Jesus, since I cannot pay
    thee,
I do adore thee, and will ever pray thee,
Think on thy pity and thy love unswerving,
Not my deserving.

SIXTH READING: Mark 15:16-20

SEVENTH READING: Mark 15:21-32

EIGHTH READING: Mark 15:33-37

    Christ candle removed or hidden, and a harsh sound.

NINTH READING: Mark 15:38-39

    A brief silence; the Christ candle is returned.

TENTH READING: Isaiah 53:4-9

HYMN: "O Sacred Head, Now Wounded"

    O Sacred Head, now wounded,
    With grief and shame weighed down,
    Now scornfully surrounded
    With thorns, thine only crown:
    How pale thou art with anguish,
    With sore abuse and scorn!
    How does that visage languish
    Which once was bright as morn!

    What thou, my Lord, hast suffered

Was all for sinners' gain;
Mine, mine was the transgression,
But thine the deadly pain.
Lo, here I fall, my Savior!
'Tis I deserve thy place;
Look on me with thy favor,
Vouchsafe to me thy grace.

What language shall I borrow
To thank thee, dearest friend,
For this thy dying sorrow,
Thy pity without end?
O make me thine forever;
And should I fainting be,
Lord, let me never, never
Outlive my love to thee.

DISMISSAL AND BLESSING:

Go in peace.
May Jesus Christ, who for our sake became obedient unto death, even death
on a cross keep you and strengthen you this night and forever. Amen.

The Passion of Our Lord According to John

(For Congregational Reading on Good Friday)

Speakers:

Narrator	Jesus	Maid
Peter	Officer	Servant
Pilate	Minor Speakers	

John 18:1–19:42

NARRATOR: Jesus . . . went forth with his disciples across the Kidron valley, where there was a garden, which he and his disciples entered. Now Judas, who betrayed him, also knew the place; for Jesus often met there with his disciples. So Judas, procuring a band of soldiers and some officers from the chief priests and the Pharisees, went there with lanterns and torches and weapons. Then Jesus, knowing all that was to befall him, came forward and said to him,

JESUS: "Whom do you seek?"

MINOR SPEAKERS: "Jesus of Nazareth."

NARRATOR: Jesus said to them,

JESUS: "I am he."

NARRATOR: Judas, who betrayed him, was standing with them. When he said to them, "I am he," they drew back and fell to the ground. Again he asked them,

JESUS: "Whom do you seek?"

MINOR SPEAKERS: "Jesus of Nazareth."

JESUS: "I told you that I am he; so, if you seek me let these men go."

NARRATOR: This was to fulfill the world which he had spoken.

JESUS: "Of those whom thou gavest me I lost not one."

NARRATOR: Then Simon Peter, having a sword, drew it and struck the high priest's slave and cut off his right ear. The slave's name was Malchus. Jesus said to Peter,

JESUS: "Put your sword into its sheath; shall I not drink the cup which the Father has given me?"

NARRATOR: So the band of soldiers and their captain and the officers of the Jews seized Jesus and bound him. First they led him to Annas; for he was the father-in-law of Caiaphas, who had given counsel to the Jews that it was expedient that one man should die for the people.

Simon Peter followed Jesus, and so did another disciple. As this disciple was known to the high priest, he entered the court of the high priest along with Jesus, while Peter stood outside at the door. So the other disciple, who was known to the high priest, went out and spoke to the maid who kept the door, and brought Peter in. The maid who kept the door said to Peter,

MAID: "Are you not also one of this man's disciples?"

PETER: "I am not."

NARRATOR: Now the servants and officers had made a charcoal fire, because it was cold, and they were standing and warming themselves; Peter also was with them, standing and warming himself.

The high priest then questioned Jesus about his disciples and his teaching. Jesus answered him.

JESUS: "I have spoken openly to the world; I have always taught in synagogues and in the temple, where all Jews come together; I have said nothing secretly. Why do you ask me? Ask those who have heard me, what I said to them; they know what I said."

NARRATOR: When he had said this, one of the officers standing by struck Jesus with his hand, saying,

OFFICER: "Is that how you answer the high priest?"

NARRATOR: Jesus answered him,

JESUS: "If I have spoken wrongly, bear witness to the wrong; but if I have spoken rightly, why do you strike me?"

NARRATOR: Annas then sent him bound to Caiaphas the high priest. Now Simon Peter was standing and warming himself.

MINOR SPEAKERS: "Are you not also one of his disciples?"

NARRATOR: He denied it and said,

PETER: "I am not."

NARRATOR: One of the servants of the high priest, a kinsman of the man whose ear Peter had cut off, asked,

SERVANT: "Did I not see you in the garden with him?

NARRATOR: Peter again denied it; and at once the cock crowed.
Then they led Jesus from the house of Caiaphas to the praetorium. It was early. They themselves did not enter the praetorium, so that they might not be defiled, but might eat the passover. So Pilate went out to them and said,

PILATE: "What accusation do you bring against this man?"

MINOR SPEAKERS: "If this man were not an evildoer, we would not have handed him over."

PILATE: "Take him yourselves and judge him by your own law."

NARRATOR: The Jews said to him,

MINOR SPEAKERS: "It is not lawful for us to put any man to death."

NARRATOR: This was to fulfil the word which Jesus had spoken to show by what death he was to die.
Pilate entered the praetorium again and called Jesus,

PILATE: "Are you the King of the Jews?"

JESUS: "Do you say this of your own accord or did others say it to you about me?"

PILATE: "Am I a Jew? Your own nation and the chief priests have handed you over to me; what have you done?"

JESUS:	"My kingship is not of this world; if my kingship were of this world, my servants would fight, that I might not be handed over to the Jews; but my kingship is not from the world."
PILATE:	"So you are a king?"
JESUS:	"You say that I am a king. For this I was born, and for this I have come into the world, to bear witness to the truth. Every one who is of the truth hears my voice."
PILATE:	"What is truth?"
NARRATOR:	After he had said this, he went out to the Jews again, and told them,
PILATE:	"I find no crime in him. But you have a custom that I should release one man for you at the Passover; will you have me release for you the King of the Jews?"
MINOR SPEAKERS:	"Not this man, but Barabbas!"
NARRATOR:	Now Barabbas was a robber. Then Pilate took Jesus and scourged him. And the soldiers plaited a crown of thorns, and put it on his head, and arrayed him in a purple robe; they came up to him, saying,
MINOR SPEAKERS:	"Hail, King of the Jews!"
NARRATOR:	And struck him with their hands. Pilate went out again, and said to them,
PILATE:	"See, I am bringing him out to you, that you may know that I find no crime in him."
NARRATOR:	So Jesus came out, wearing the crown of thorns and the purple robe.
PILATE:	"Behold the man!"
NARRATOR:	When the chief priests and the officers saw him, they cried out,
PEOPLE:	**"Crucify him, crucify him!"**
PILATE:	"Take him yourselves and crucify him, for I find no crime in him."

NARRATOR: The Jews answered him,

PEOPLE: **"We have a law, and by that law he ought to die, because he has made himself the Son of God."**

NARRATOR: When Pilate heard these words, he was the more afraid; he entered the praetorium again and said to Jesus,

PILATE: "Where are you from?"

NARRATOR: But Jesus gave no answer. Pilate therefore said to him,

PILATE: "You will not speak to me? Do you now know that I have power to release you, and power to crucify you?"

JESUS: "You would have no power over me unless it had been given you from above; therefore he who delivered me to you has the greater sin."

NARRATOR: Upon this Pilate sought to release him, but the Jews cried out.

MINOR
SPEAKERS: "If you release this man, you are not Caesar's friend; every one who makes himself a king sets himself against Caesar."

NARRATOR: When Pilate heard these words, he brought Jesus out and sat down on the judgment seat at a place called The Pavement and in Hebrew, Gabbatha. Now it was the day of Preparation of the Passover; it was about the sixth hour. He said to the Jews,

PILATE: "Behold your King!"

PEOPLE: **"Away with him, away with him, crucify him!"**

PILATE: "Shall I crucify your King?"

NARRATOR: The chief priests answered,

MINOR
SPEAKERS: "We have no king but Caesar."

NARRATOR: Then he handed him over to them to be crucified. So they took Jesus, and he went out, bearing his own cross, to the place called the place of a skull, which is called in Hebrew Golgotha. There they crucified him, and with him two others, one on either side, and Jesus between them. Pilate also wrote a title and put it on the cross; it read, "Jesus of Nazareth, the King of the Jews." Many of the Jews read this title, for the place where Jesus was crucified was near the city; and it was written in Hebrew, in Latin, and in Greek. The chief priests of the Jews then said to Pilate,

MINOR SPEAKERS: "Do not write, 'The King of the Jews,' but 'This man said, I am King of the Jews.' "

PILATE: "What I have written I have written."

NARRATOR: When the soldiers had crucified Jesus they took his garments and made four parts, one for each soldier; also his tunic. But his tunic was without seam, woven from top to bottom; so they said to one another,

MINOR SPEAKERS: "Let us not tear it, but cast lots for it to see whose it shall be."

NARRATOR: This was to fulfill the scripture. "They parted my garments among them and for my clothing they cast lots."

So the soldiers did this. But standing by the cross of Jesus were his mother, and his mother's sister, Mary the wife of Clopas, and Mary Magdalene. When Jesus saw his mother, and the disciple whom he loved standing near, he said to his mother,

JESUS: "Women, behold your son!"

NARRATOR: Then he said to the disciple,

JESUS: "Behold your mother!"

NARRATOR: And from that hour the disciple took her to his own home.

After this Jesus, knowing that all was now finished, said (to fulfill the scripture),

JESUS: "I thirst."

NARRATOR: A bowl of vinegar stood there; so they put a sponge full of the vinegar of hyssop and held it to his mouth. When Jesus had received the vinegar, he said,

JESUS: "It is finished"

NARRATOR: and he bowed his head and gave up his spirit.

Since it was the day of Preparation, in order to prevent the bodies from remaining on the cross on the sabbath (for that sabbath was a high day), the Jews asked Pilate that their legs might be broken, and that they might be taken away. So the soldiers came and broke the legs of the first, and of the other who had been crucified with him; but when they came to Jesus and saw that he was already dead, they did not break his legs. But one of the soldiers pierced his side with a spear; and at once there came out blood and water. He who saw it has borne witness—his testimony is true, and he knows that he tells the truth—that you also may believe. For these things took place that the scripture might be fulfilled.

PEOPLE: **"Not a bone of him shall be broken."**

NARRATOR: And again another scripture says,

PEOPLE: **"They shall look on him whom they have pierced."**

NARRATOR: After this Joseph of Arimathea, who was a disciple of Jesus, but secretly, for fear of the Jews, asked Pilate that he might take away the body of Jesus, and Pilate gave him leave. So he came and took away his body. Nicodemus also, who had at first come to him by night, came bringing a mixture of myrrh and aloes, about a hundred pounds weight. They took the body of Jesus, and bound it in linen cloths with the spices, as is the burial custom of the Jews. Now in the place where he was crucified there was a garden, and in the garden a new tomb where no one had ever been laid. So because of the Jewish day of Preparation, as the tomb was close at hand, they laid Jesus there.

The Passion of Our Lord According to Matthew

(For Congregational Reading on Passion/Palm Sunday)

Speakers:

Narrator	Witness	Jeremiah
Judas	High Priest	Pilate
Jesus	First Maid	Pilate's Wife
Peter	Second Maid	Minor Speakers

Matthew 26:14–27:66

NARRATOR: Then one of the twelve, who was called Judas Iscariot, went to the chief priest and said,

JUDAS: "What will you give me if I deliver him to you?"

NARRATOR: And they paid him thirty pieces of silver. And from that moment he sought an opportunity to betray him.

Now on the first day of Unleavened Bread the disciples came to Jesus, saying,

MINOR SPEAKERS: "Where will you have us prepare for you to eat the passover?

NARRATOR: And the disciples did as Jesus directed them, and they prepared the passover.

When it was evening he sat at table with the twelve disciples; and as they were eating, he said,

JESUS: "Truly, I say to you, one of you will betray me."

NARRATOR: And they were very sorrowful, and began to say to him one after another.

MINOR SPEAKERS: "Is it I, Lord?" (*May be repeated*)

NARRATOR: He answered,

JESUS: "He who has dipped his hand in the dish with me, will betray me. The Son of man goes as it is written of him, but woe to that man by whom the Son of man is betrayed! It would have been better for that man if he had not been born."

NARRATOR: Judas, who betrayed him, said,

JUDAS: "Is it I, Master?"

NARRATOR: He said to him,

JESUS: "You have said so."

NARRATOR: Now as they were eating, Jesus took bread, and blessed, and broke it, and gave it to the disciples and said,

JESUS: "Take, eat; this is my body."

NARRATOR: And he took a cup, and when he had given thanks he gave it to them, saying,

JESUS: "Drink of it, all of you; for this is my blood of the covenant, which is poured out for many for the forgiveness of sins. I tell you I shall not drink again of this fruit of the vine until that day when I drink it new with you in my Father's kingdom."

NARRATOR: And when they had sung a hymn, they went out to the Mount of Olives. Then Jesus said to them,

JESUS: "You will all fall away because of me this night; for it is written, 'I will strike the shepherd, and the sheep of the flock will be scattered.' But after I am raised up, I will go before you to Galilee."

NARRATOR: Peter declared to him,

PETER: "Though they all fall away because of you, I will never fall away."

NARRATOR: Jesus said to him,

JESUS: "Truly, I say to you, this very night, before the cock crows, you will deny me three times."

NARRATOR: Peter said to him,

PETER: "Even if I must die with you, I will not deny you."

NARRATOR: And so said all the disciples. Then Jesus went with them to a place called Gethsemane, and he said to his disciples,

JESUS:	"Sit here, while I go yonder and pray."
NARRATOR:	And taking with him Peter and the two sons of Zebedee, he began to be sorrowful and troubled. Then he said to them,
JESUS:	"My soul is very sorrowful, even to death; remain here, and watch with me."
NARRATOR:	And going a little farther he fell on his face and prayed,
JESUS:	"My Father, if it be possible, let this cup pass from me; nevertheless, not as I will, but as thou wilt."
NARRATOR:	And he came to the disciples and found them sleeping; and he said to Peter,
JESUS:	"So, could you not watch with me one hour? Watch and pray that you may not enter into temptation; the spirit is willing, but the flesh is weak."
NARRATOR:	Again, for the second time, he went away and prayed,
JESUS:	"My Father, if this cannot pass unless I drink it, thy will be done."
NARRATOR:	And again he came and found them sleeping, for their eyes were heavy. So, leaving them again, he went away and prayed for the third time, saying the same words. Then he came to the disciples and said to them,
JESUS:	"Are you still sleeping and taking your rest? Behold, the hour is at hand, and the Son of man is betrayed into the hands of sinners. Rise, let us be going; see, my betrayer is at hand."
NARRATOR:	While is was still speaking, Judas came, one of the twelve, and with him a great crowd with swords and clubs, from the chief priests and the elders of the people. Now the betrayer had given them a sign, saying,
JUDAS:	"This one I shall kiss is the man; seize him."
NARRATOR:	And he came up to Jesus at once and said,
JUDAS:	"Hail Master!"
NARRATOR:	And he kissed him. Jesus said to him,
JESUS:	"Friend, why are you here?"

NARRATOR: Then they came up and laid hands on Jesus and seized him. And behold, one of those who were with Jesus stretched out his hand and drew his sword, and struck the slave of the high priest, and cut off his ear. Then Jesus said to him,

JESUS: "Put your sword back into its place; for all who take the sword will perish by the sword. Do you think that I cannot appeal to my Father, and he will at once send me more than twelve legions of angels? But how then should the scriptures be fulfilled, that it must be so?"

NARRATOR: At that hour Jesus said to the crowds,

JESUS: "Have you come out as against a robber, with swords and clubs to capture me? Day after day I sat in the temple teaching, and you did not seize me. But all this has taken place, that the scriptures of the prophets might be fulfilled."

NARRATOR: Then all the disciples forsook him and fled.

Then those who had seized Jesus led him to Caiaphas the high priest, where the scribes and the elders had gathered. But Peter followed him at a distance, as far as the courtyard of the high priest, and going inside he sat with the guards to see the end. Now the chief priest and the whole council sought false testimony against Jesus that they might put him to death, but they found none, though many false witnesses came forward. At last two came forward and said,

WITNESS: "This fellow said, 'I am able to destroy the temple of God, and to build it in three days.' "

NARRATOR: And the high priest stood up and said,

HIGH PRIEST: "I adjure you by the living God, tell us if you are the Christ, the Son of God."

NARRATOR: Jesus said to him,

JESUS: "You have said so. But I tell you, hereafter you will see the Son of man seated at the right hand of Power, and coming on the clouds of heaven."

NARRATOR: Then the high priest tore his robes, and said,

HIGH PRIEST:	"He has uttered blasphemy. Why do we still need witnesses? You have now heard his blasphemy. What is your judgment?"
PEOPLE:	**"He serves death."**
NARRATOR:	Then they spat in his face, and struck him; and some slapped him, saying,
PEOPLE:	**"Prophesy to us, you Christ! Who is it that struck you?"**
NARRATOR:	Now Peter was sitting outside in the courtyard. And a maid came up to him, and said,
FIRST MAID:	"You also were with Jesus the Galilean."
NARRATOR:	But he denied it before them all, saying,
PETER:	"I do not know what you mean."
NARRATOR:	And when he went out to the porch, another maid saw him, and she said to the bystanders,
SECOND MAID:	"This man was with Jesus of Nazareth."
NARRATOR:	And again he denied it with an oath,
PETER:	"I do not know the man."
NARRATOR:	After a little while the bystanders came up and said to Peter,
PEOPLE:	**"Certainly you are also one of them, for your accent betrays you."**
NARRATOR:	Then he began to invoke a curse on himself and to swear.
PETER:	"I do not know the man."
NARRATOR:	And immediately the cock crowed. And Peter remembered the saying of Jesus, "Before the cock crows you will deny me three times." And he went and wept bitterly. When morning came, all the chief priests and the elders of the people took counsel against Jesus to put him to death; and they bound him and led him away and delivered him to Pilate the governor. When Judas, his betrayer, saw that he was condemned, he

repented and brought back the thirty pieces of silver to the chief priest and the elders, saying,

JUDAS: "I have sinned in betraying innocent blood."

MINOR SPEAKERS: "What is that to us? See to it yourself."

NARRATOR: And throwing down the pieces of silver in the temple, he departed; and he went and hanged himself. But the chief priests, taking the pieces of silver, said,

MINOR SPEAKERS: "It is not lawful to put them into the treasury, since they are blood money."

NARRATOR: So they took counsel, and bought with them the potter's field, to bury strangers in. Therefore that field has been called the Field of Blood to this day. Then was fulfilled what had been spoken by the prophet Jeremiah, saying,

JEREMIAH: "And they took the thirty pieces of silver, the price of him on whom a price had been set by some of the sons of Israel, and they gave them for the potter's field, as the Lord directed me."

NARRATOR: Now Jesus stood before the governor; and the governor asked him,

PILATE: "Are you the King of the Jews?"

JESUS: "You have said so."

NARRATOR: But when he was accused by the chief priests and elders, he made no answer. Then Pilate said to him,

PILATE: "Do you not hear how many things they testify against you?"

NARRATOR: But he gave him no answer, not even to a single charge; so that the governor wondered greatly.

Now at the feast the governor was accustomed to release for the crowd any one prisoner whom they wanted. And they had then a notorious prisoner, called Barabbas. So when they had gathered, Pilate said to them,

PILATE: "Whom do you want me to release for you, Barabbas or Jesus who is called Christ?"

NARRATOR: For he knew that it was out of envy that they had delivered him up. Besides, while he was sitting on the judgment seat, his wife sent word to him,

PILATE'S WIFE: "Have nothing to do with that righteous man, for I have suffered much over him today in a dream."

NARRATOR: Now the chief priests and elders persuaded the people to ask for Barabbas and destroy Jesus. The governor again said to them,

PILATE: "Which of the two do you want me to release for you?"

PEOPLE: **"Barabbas."**

NARRATOR: Pilate said to them,

PILATE: "Then what shall I do with Jesus who is called Christ?"

PEOPLE: **"Let him be crucified."**

PILATE: "Why, what evil has he done?"

NARRATOR: But they shouted all the more,

PEOPLE: **"Let him be crucified!"**

NARRATOR: So when Pilate saw that he was gaining nothing, but rather that a riot was beginning, he took water and washed his hands before the crowd, saying,

PILATE: "I am innocent of this man's blood; see to it yourselves."

NARRATOR: Then he released for them Barabbas, and having scourged Jesus, delivered him to be crucified. Then the soldiers of the governor took Jesus into the praetorium, and they gathered the whole battalion before him. And they stripped him and put a scarlet robe upon him, and plaiting a crown of thorns they put it on his head, and put a reed in his right hand. And kneeling before him they mocked him, saying,

PEOPLE: **"Hail, King of the Jews!"**

NARRATOR: And they spat upon him, and took the reed and struck him on the head. And when they had mocked him, they stripped him of the robe, and put his own clothes on him, and led him away to crucify him.

As they went out, they came upon a man of Cyrene, Simon by name; this man they compelled to carry his cross. And when they came to a place called Golgotha (which means the place of a skull), they offered him wine to drink, mingled with gall; but when he tasted it, he would not drink it. And when they had crucified him, they divided his garments among them by casting lots; then they sat down and kept watch over him there. And over his head they put the charge against him, which read, "This is Jesus the King of the Jews." Then two robbers were crucified with him, one on the right and one on the left. And those who passed by derided him, wagging their heads and saying,

PEOPLE: **"You who would destroy the temple and build it in three days, save yourself! If you are the Son of God, come down from the cross."**

NARRATOR: So also the chief priests, with the scribes and elders, mocked him, saying,

MINOR
SPEAKERS: "He saved others, he cannot save himself. He is the king of Israel; let him come down now from the cross, and we will believe in him. He trusts in God; let God deliver him now, if he desires him, for he said, 'I am the Son of God.' "

NARRATOR: And the robbers who were crucified with him also reviled him in the same way. Now from the sixth hour there was darkness over all the land until the ninth hour. And about the ninth hour Jesus cried with a loud voice.

JESUS: "Eli, Eli, la'ma sabach-tha'ni?
My God, my God, why hast thou forsaken me?"

MINOR
SPEAKERS: "This man is calling Elijah."

NARRATOR: And one of them at once ran and took a sponge, filled it with vinegar, and put it on a reed, and gave it to him to drink.

MINOR
SPEAKERS: "Wait, let us see whether Elijah will come to save him."

NARRATOR: And Jesus cried again with a loud voice and yielded up his spirit.

(pause)

And behold, the curtain of the temple was torn in two, from top to bottom; and the earth shook, and the rocks were split; the tombs also were opened, and many bodies of the saints who had fallen asleep were raised, and coming out of the tombs after his resurrection they went into the holy city and appeared to many. When the centurion and those who were with him, keeping watch over Jesus, saw the earthquake and what took place, they were filled with awe, and said,

MINOR SPEAKERS: "Truly this was the Son of God!"

NARRATOR: There were also many women there, looking on from afar, who had followed Jesus from Galilee, ministering to him; among whom were Mary Magdalene, and Mary the mother of James and Joseph, and the mother of the sons of Zebedee.

When it was evening, there came a rich man from Arimathea, named Joseph, who also was a disciple of Jesus. He went to Pilate and asked for the body of Jesus. Then Pilate ordered it to be given to him. And Joseph took the body, and wrapped it in a clean linen shroud, and laid it in his own new tomb, which he had hewn in the rock; and he rolled a great stone to the door of the tomb, and departed. Mary Magdalene and the other Mary were there, sitting opposite the sepulchre.

Next day—that is, after the day of Preparation, the chief priests and the Pharisees gathered before Pilate and said,

MINOR SPEAKERS: "Sir, we remember how that impostor said, while he was still alive, 'After three days I will rise again.' Therefore order the sepulchre to be made secure until the third day, lest his disciples go and steal him away, and tell the people, 'He has risen from the dead,' and the last fraud will be worse than the first."

NARRATOR: Pilate said to them,

PILATE: "You have a guard of soldiers; go make it as secure as you can."

NARRATOR: So they went and made the sepulchre secure by sealing the stone and setting a guard.

A Service for a Church Anniversary or Homecoming

CALL TO WORSHIP

Unless the Lord builds the house those who build it labor in vain. Unless the Lord watches over the city the watchman stays awake in vain.

HYMN: "And Are We Yet Alive"

INVOCATION

O Lord of all days, we thank you for time to reflect. We look backwards now, over the year behind us, and see there evidence of your leading. Help us to look ahead, in confidence that you will provide work for our hands. Thank you for the friendships that have grown up between us as we have worked and worshiped together. May this church fulfill the purposes of your Kingdom here on earth. Speak to us now, Lord, through hymns and scripture, through meditations, through your voice in our hearts. Amen.

UNISON PRAYER

Help each of us, gracious God,
    to live in such magnanimity and restraint
that the Head of the church may never have
cause to say to any one of us,
    "This is my body, broken by you." Amen.
                                        A Prayer from China

WORDS OF ASSURANCE

The past is finished and gone, everything has become fresh and new.

THE LORD'S PRAYER

SCRIPTURE LESSONS: Genesis 28:10-16
                               Ephesians 4

AFFIRMATION OF FAITH: The Apostle's Creed

GLORIA PATRI

LITANY

Save us, O God from living in the past and from resting on the work of those who have gone before us. Let us find a new beginning and a new vision, that we may know our task in this place and in this world today.

O God, give us vision.

Enable us to accept the responsibility of our freedom, the burden of our privilege, and so conduct ourselves as to set an example for those who will follow after.

O God, give us courage.

Spare us from the pride that separates and excludes. Defend us from the ignorance that perpetuates injustice and from the indifference that causes hearts to break.

O God, give us understanding.

Being united in this church, sharing in the great mission that you have set before us, let us find in your church a prod to our imagination, a shock to our laziness, and a source of power in doing your will.

O God, give us strength.

O God, who has given us minds to know you and hearts to love you: send your spirit upon us, make us one, and free us to serve you.

Amen.

HYMN: "What Gift Can We Bring"

SERMON

OFFERTORY

PRAYER OF DEDICATION

O God, you have honored us by calling us into your church. In that calling you have promised to be our guide and our strength. As we look ahead we are deeply aware of our need for your presence. The tasks are large and the volunteers few. It would be easy for us to become weary, cynical, and bitter. Help us to keep our eyes on Jesus who has brought this church to the place it is today. Pour forth your spirit upon us. We dedicate ourselves anew to this church, to your church universal, and to you. May we become a more worthy instrument in the realization of your kingdom.

CHURCH REMINISCENCE

HYMN: "O God, Our Help in Ages Past"

BENEDICTION

A Service for Mother's Day

PRELUDE

A TRIBUTE TO MOTHERHOOD

Today is Mother's Day. It is a day to give honor and recognition to our mothers, and to those who are just like mothers to us. It is a day to thank them for their love, care, and support throughout the years.

Mothers are special. They wipe runny noses, bandage scraped knees, and dry away tears. They fix broken toys, drive us everywhere we need to go, and still have time to make our favorite treat.

Mothers are special. They cried when we went off to kindergarten, they cried when we went off to college. They cried when we were ready to enter the "real" world beyond school. They cried when we got married, when we had our first child, when we left after a holiday visit.

Mothers are special. We take them wherever they need to go, thread the needle for them, and make sure that someone is always nearby. We do the scrubbing, the shopping, and the dishes. We show them how to work the remote control.

On this special day, we honor all mothers—whether they are our biological or spiritual mothers.

HYMN: "In the Circle of Each Home"

SCRIPTURE READING: Proverbs 31:10-31; 1 Corinthians 13

HYMN: "A Christian Home"

OFFERING AND DOXOLOGY

MEDITATION

In 1910 Agnes Gonxha Bejaxhiu was born into an Albanian family living in Skopje, Yugoslavia. Perhaps you are wondering who she is and why we are thinking of her today on Mother's Day. Agnes Foxha Bejaxhiu never became a biological mother, but the name she is known by today, Mother Theresa, is familiar throughout the world.

Mother Theresa is the very embodiment of our memories of our own mothers. She saw what had to be done and did it. Can we not say that about our mothers? She doesn't expect recognition. She sees the work, not herself, as important. Mother Theresa put love into action. So do our mothers. Loving us is not always easy, yet our mothers never give their love for us a second thought. They simply do it. And it is that example that allows us to grow in love both to God and to others.

Many of us wear flowers today in recognition or in memory of our mothers. We have sent them cards, we'll take them gifts, maybe we will cook for them, or take them out for a meal. But today is a day for much more than candy and flowers and cards. It is a day to celebrate love. The best way we can honor our mothers today is to share the love of God, the love instilled in us by our mothers, and others—not just today, but every day. Let us, like Mother Theresa and our own mother, put love into action.

HYMN: "Pass it On"

BENEDICTION

A Service for Women's Day

PRELUDE

OPENING HYMN: "Great is Thy Faithfulness"

CALL TO WORSHIP:

Seek the Lord while he may be found,
    call upon him while he is near.

**let the wicked forsake their way,
    and the unrighteous their thoughts;**

let them return to the Lord, that he
    may have mercy on them,

and to our God, for he will abundantly pardon.

Isaiah 55:6-7 NRSV

WELCOME

Honored guests, from the very beginning of time, from Eve to the present day, women have played a significant role in the life of the church. Today we honor and applaud the women of this church, for, without them, it is safe to say this church would not exist! Proverbs 31:10 states, "Who can find a virtuous woman? for her price is far above rubies." The "rubies" set in the crown of this church all glow as reminders that God has blessed us.

We read in Galatians, "When the fullness of time was come, God sent forth his Son, *made of a woman,* made under the law, To redeem them that were under the law, that we might receive the adoption of heirs" (Galatians 4:4-5, emphasis added). It was through a woman that the Son of God came to earth, and it is in his name and the name of all women that I welcome you to this celebration of Women's Day.

HYMN: "Getting Used to the Family of God"

SCRIPTURE READING: Proverbs 31:10-31; 2 Timothy 3-14

OFFERING AND DOXOLOGY

MEDITATION

HYMN: "There's a Church Within Us, O Lord"

BENEDICTION

A Service for Father's Day

PRELUDE

WELCOME

Welcome to our service of celebration on this Father's Day. We come to honor these fathers who taught us skills and tenderness, played with us and worked for us, loved us and advised us. Today we say thanks to those fathers who worked to provide more than shelter, who provided a home for their children. Today we honor those fathers who came with their families to church, instead of dropping them off. Today we celebrate those fathers whose love for their children is modeled on God's love for all children. Today we thank God for loving fathers, and for all those men, though not our biological fathers, who have cared for us.

In Ephesians we read, "Honor thy father and mother; which is the first commandment with promise; that it may be well with thee, and thou mayest live long on the earth. And, ye fathers, provoke not your children to wrath: but bring them up in the nurture and admonition of the Lord" (Ephesians 6:2-4 KJV). We are glad to be here to honor those men who nurture this church, and on behalf of those men and all gathered here, I bid you welcome.

HYMN: "Faith of Our Fathers"

SCRIPTURE READING: 1 Corinthians 13; Proverbs 23:22-25, 24:3-5

HYMN: "A Christian Home"

OFFERING AND DOXOLOGY

MEDITATION

In 1840 Joseph de Vuester was born in Temeloo, Belgium. Later he became known as Father Damien, a Roman Catholic priest known throughout the world for his work with the leper colony on the island of Molokai.

Father Damien never became a biological father, but in his example we see the very embodiment of our own fathers. Father Damien saw what had to be done and did it. Can we not say that about our own fathers? He never expected recognition. He saw the work, not himself as important. Father Damien put love into action. So do our fathers. Loving us is not always easy, yet our fathers never give their love for us a second thought. They simply do it. And it is that example that allows us to grow in love both to God and to others.

Many of us wear flowers today in recognition or in memory of our fathers. We have sent them cards, we'll take them gifts, perhaps we have planned to take them out for a meal. But today is a day for much more than flowers and meals and cards. It is a day to celebrate love. The best way we can honor our fathers today is to share the love of God, the love instilled in us by our fathers, with others—not just today, but every day. Let us, like Father Damien and our own fathers, put love into action.

HYMN: "Pass it On"

BENEDICTION

A Service for Men's Day

PRELUDE

HYMN: "Great Is Thy Faithfulness"

CALL TO WORSHIP

Seek the Lord while he may be found,
   call upon him while he is near.

**let the wicked forsake their way,
   and the unrighteous their thoughts.**

let them return to the Lord, that he
   may have mercy on them

and to our God, for he will abundantly pardon.

Isaiah 55:6-7 NRSV

WELCOME

I am delighted to welcome you here today. Every man here is outstanding; not perhaps by the world's standards, but by God's standards of love and service. Genesis tells us that "the Lord God formed man of the dust of the ground, and breathed into his nostrils the breath of life; and man became a living soul" (Genesis 2:7 KJV). Our very souls are delighted to be here at this celebration today and I bid you welcome.

HYMN: "Getting Used to the Family of God"

READING:

The Bridge Builder

An old man going a lone highway
Came at evening cold and gray,
To a chasm vast and deep and wide
Without a bridge to span the tide;
The old man crossed in twilight dim,
The sullen stream held no fear for him.
He turned when on the other side
And built a bridge to span the tide.

"Old man," said a pilgrim near,

"You waste your strength with building here.
Your journey ends with ending day.
You ne'er again will pass this way.
Your feet no more must need pass o'er
This sullen stream with sullen road.
You've crossed the chasm deep and wide.
Why build this bridge at eventide?"

The old man turned his hoary head.
"Friend, in the path I've come," he said,
"There followeth after me today
A youth whose feet must pass this way.
This chasm that's as naught to me
To that fair youth may a pitfall be.
He, too, must cross in twilight dim—
Good friend, I build the bridge for him.
                    Will Allen Dromgoole

SCRIPTURE READING: Psalm 16; Hebrews 13:1-18

OFFERING AND DOXOLOGY

MEDITATION

HYMN: "Rise Up, O Men of God"

BENEDICTION

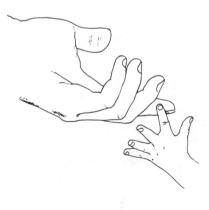

A Service for Children's Day

(This service may also be adapted for Promotion Day. Promotion of classes may take place at any time.)

PRELUDE

OPENING HYMN: "I Sing a Song of the Saints of God"

CALL TO WORSHIP

Children's Day

Children's Day! Most loved of all
In every childish heart;
It brings to mind a Savior's call
And blessed memories start;
We see the Christ of Galilee
With hand on tiny head—
"O let the children come to me,"
The Savior sweetly said.

Children's Day! O may we keep
This festival of our own
With pledge so solemn and so deep
To reach the Father's throne;
May we resolve in earnest ways
To give to Christ our all;
We hear the words of olden days—
We'll heed the loving call.

PRESCHOOLER'S HYMN: "Jesus Loves Me"

YOUTH CHOIR HYMN: "Pass It On"

UNISON READING: (by children from older elementary classes): Psalm 100; Matthew 5:1-12

(If promotions are to take place, during the presentation of certificates and/or Bibles, congregation and/or choir may sing "Open My Eyes, That I May See;" "O Word of God Incarnate" or other appropriate hymns.)

PASTORAL PRAYER

LORD'S PRAYER

OFFERING AND DOXOLOGY

SCRIPTURE READING (by a young person): Acts 2:1-7, 16-17

MEDITATION

HYMN: "Come, Christians, Join to Sing"

BENEDICTION

"The Lord bless you and keep you: The Lord make his face to shine upon you, and be gracious to you: The Lord lift up his countenance upon you, and give you peace" (Numbers 6:24-26). Amen.

A Service for Rally Day

PRELUDE

CALL TO WORSHIP

O God, open our lips.

And our mouths shall show forth your praise.

Praise the Lord.

HYMN OF PRAISE

PRAYER OF INVOCATION

In unison:
  O God, grant that we may love you with all our heart, with all our mind, and with all our strength. Grant that we may love our neighbors according to your grace and live at peace with all people. Cleanse our hearts of envy, impatience, and ill will. Fill us with kindness and compassion that we may rejoice in the happiness and success of others and share with them in their sorrows, So we may live and work together as your children in the spirit of Jesus Christ our Lord. Amen.

THE LORD'S PRAYER

SCRIPTURE LESSON: Jonah 3 and 4

PASTORAL PRAYER

PRAYER HYMN: "Dear Lord and Father of Mankind"

OFFERING

DOXOLOGY

SERMON: (Suggested topic, "The Church As a Family")

LITANY OF DEDICATION

To be entered into by all in the mood of prayer.
And God formed man of the dust of the ground, and breathed into his nostrils the breath of life. Likewise God fashioned woman from the rib of a man; and they became living souls.

That you made us for yourself and that our hearts are restless until they rest in you, we thank you, O God.

The God that made the world and all things in it gives to all life and breath; and God made from one all the nations of people to dwell on the face of the earth.

That you have set your divine life in all life, we thank you, O God.

God set the solitary in families, and said to Abraham, In your seed shall all the families of the earth be blessed.

For the rich heritage of parenthood and the Christ-likeness of childhood, we thank you, O God.

Train up children in the way they should go, and even when they are old they will not depart from it. And Jesus set a child in their midst.

For the fresh revelation of yourself in each little child, and for the bonds of love which bind childhood, youth, and maturity together—we thank you, O God.

Jesus looked round about on them that sat about him and said, Behold my mother and my brethren! For whosoever shall do the will of God, the same is my brother, and sister, and mother.

That belonging to one family is so clearly shown in the Scriptures and in the life of your Son—we thank you, O God.

Now are we the children of God, and members one of another.

All: To the divine relationship as children of our Heavenly Father, we dedicate ourselves, our souls and bodies to be living sacrifices unto you, O God. For their sakes—for all your children—we consecrate ourselves gladly to teach and willingly to learn the Way, the Truth, and the Life, that your whole family may be redeemed through Jesus Christ. Amen.

HYMN: "Joyful, Joyful, We Adore Thee"

BENEDICTION

POSTLUDE

World Communion Sunday

GATHERING

GREETING

CALL TO WORSHIP

PASTOR: Come from the East, come from the West. Come from all corners of the globe.

PEOPLE: Come sisters and brothers. Come home for the family feast.

PASTOR: The one who created us, the one who loves us, has prepared a meal for us.

PEOPLE: Come and be nourished by the love that sustains.

ALL: We give thanks for the opportunity to come home, and to come together and worship.

HYMN OF PRAISE

OLD TESTAMENT Exodus 16:2-4, 13-18

PRAYER OF CONFESSION

O God of Creation, so often we are too short-sighted to see the abundance you have given us. We worry, forgetting your great supply. We fall prey to restrictions on and divisions of your family. We forget that there is enough for all.

As we gather in your presence this morning, open your minds and hearts to your whole creation. Teach us to be healers and lovers and justice-seekers. Lift us beyond our limits to your great plenty, that we may grow wiser in your Spirit-knowledge. Amen.

WORDS OF ASSURANCE

When three or four gather in the Spirit, God is present—hearing, receiving, responding.

A TIME OF PRAYER FOR THE WORLD

(Each concern is followed by moments of silent prayer.)

Let us turn our prayerful meditations to the others in our world:
    —Our Church and all who enter here . . .

—The people of our nation and its leaders . . .

—The people and leaders of the world, particularly where hunger, poverty, and political unrest prevail . . .

—Our denomination and the Church Universal . . .

O Lord, draw us all together in this great world of yours. Heal our divisions, calm our fears, and enlighten our ignorance. As we gather around your table this morning, bind us with all our sisters and brothers everywhere. Unite us in your love. *(All join in the Lord's Prayer.)*

EPISTLE Revelation 21:5-7

OFFERING with Doxology

HYMN OF PREPARATION

GOSPEL John 21:15-17

SERMON

Look around. Whom do we exclude? The emphasis for today is unity in Christ. God makes no distinctions among people. Why do we? Concentrate on including all people—include those who are "outcast" by race, income level, marital status, or other circumstances. Look at current hot spots—nations or areas with problems at the moment.

AFFIRMATION OF FAITH

I believe in the One who gave order to chaos and breathed life into the universe. I believe that this One remains fully committed to and involved with the world.

I believe in the One who entered into the day-to-day life of the universe. I believe that this one lived and walked the earth as a healer, a guide, and a liberator from the limitations of life, even the limitation called death.

I believe in the One who dwells in me, as a source of calm, strength, and wisdom. I believe in the One who dwells in each of us, drawing us closer to the reign of God.

I believe in the church as the Host of Creation, inviting all into the pattern of God's patchwork plan. Amen.

COMMUNION HYMN

CELEBRATION OF THE HOLY MEAL

INVITATION

On this day especially, when the barriers between people are struck down. God invites you to join Christians everywhere at the holy banquet table.

PRAYER OF CONSECRATION

Author of all life, in whose image each of us is made, hear our prayer of thanks for all your good gifts. You chose our ancestors and made them your people. In the deserts of our lives, you have been with us. You meet us on the mountains and go with us through the valleys. You supply our every need.

In Jesus Christ, your love for all was made evident. He ate with outcasts, strengthened the weary, walked with the lonely. He offered his life on our behalf: He was crucified, died, and rose victorious, even over death.

On the night Jesus was to be betrayed, he gathered his friends from all walks of life, wishing to share his last meal with those he loved. He took a common loaf of bread and transformed it into the bread of life.

He broke the bread and shared it, saying, "Whenever you eat this, it will bless you. This bread represents my body, which is broken for you. Take some and eat it."

Then he poured the drink and blessed it, saying, "Drink this, all of you. It represents my blood offered for you. Remember that your sins are forgiven."

Spirit, send your power upon these gifts, your bread and your cup. Bless them and your people all around the world. As we partake of these common elements, unite our spirits in love for you, and our hearts in love for one another. In the name of the Creator, our Redeemer and Sustainer, **Amen.**

PRAYER OF THANKSGIVING

We thank you, God, for making one people out of many. Thank you for your love in Jesus, who invites us to his table, a people forgiven. Look upon us as we leave this feast, that the union we have shared here not be forgotten, but be used to strengthen our bonds with all your people. **Amen.**

SPECIAL OFFERING with Charge and Prayer

In joyful response to God's good gifts, let us now share with one another throughout the world.

God, accept these gifts as symbols of our love for you. On this World Communion Sunday, use these gifts to unite your family all around the world. **Amen.**

HYMN OF DEDICATION

BENEDICTION

A Service for Laity Sunday

PRELUDE

CHORAL CALL: "I'm Goin'a Sing When the Spirit Says Sing" (Choir and congregation together. Right side sings verse 1, left side verse 2, all sing verse 4.)

GREETING:

We come together as individuals, unique unto ourselves.

We come together seeking the Spirit's touch.

Our faith journeys intertwine in this sacred place.

And we grow closer together in our lives here.

We are a congregation, gathered in God's name.

Together, our faith makes us strong.

HYMN: "Jesus Calls Us"

SCRIPTURE: Genesis 1:1-13; 1:27–2:2

PRAYERS OF THE PEOPLE

(Moments of silence, Prayer of Intercession, and the Lord's Prayer)

EPISTLE: 1 Corinthians 12:12-31

OFFERING WITH DOXOLOGY

JOYS AND CONCERNS/PASSING OF THE PEACE

JUMBLE PRAYER

The Jumble Prayer helps make the point that God hears the prayers of each and every person who prays. Each of us will fill in the blanks (aloud) with our own response. Though the result may sound jumbled to us, we can be assured that God hears each of us clearly. The leader reads a line of the prayers, we each respond together.

Dear God, hear the voices of your people as we bring our prayers for others:
We pray for someone who is ill _____
We pray for a friend who is troubled _____
We pray for a child who needs your guidance _____
We pray for someone who is facing tough times _____
We pray for someone who is far away _____

We pray that the words of our mouths and the meditations of our hearts will be acceptable in your sight. In Jesus' name, Amen.

GOSPEL: Matthew 25:14-30

MEDITATION

HYMN: "Wonderful Words of Life"

BENEDICTION

DISMISSAL: The Congregation

"God Be With You Till We Meet Again"

An Order for the Reaffirmation of Marriage

Note: *This order contains a flexible worship service which focuses on the reaffirmation of marriage. Incorporated in this service is a ceremony for the reaffirmation of wedding vows.*

PRELUDE

WORDS OF WELCOME AND EXPLANATION:

(Here the pastor may share the purposes of reaffirmation, answer some of the common questions, assure the dignity of those who cannot participate, and note the relationship between God's family, family units, and Christian marriage.)

RESPONSIVE AFFIRMATION OF THE FAMILY:

Let us affirm our families.

For they can bring out what is good in life.

Let us affirm young people.

Children and Youth: **We grow and find love in our families.**

Let us affirm adults.

Adults: **Praise God for our families and the ties that bind us together.**

Let us all affirm our families.

For each of our families, we give thanks to God, who brings and keeps families together.

HYMN: *(Choose a hymn that stresses the family of God.)*

PASTORAL PRAYER FOR FAMILY LIVING

SCRIPTURE READINGS: Eccl. 4:9-12; Matt. 19:4-6; 1 Cor. 13.

MEDITATION:

(These several affirmations about marriage and family may be read or used as meditation starters.)

    1. A covenant is a solemn promise, made verbally or with symbolic action, which formally binds both parties. In the long span of history of the Old and

New Testaments, covenants have met deep human needs in both religion and law. We value the Ten Commandments of the Old Testament as God's covenant with the people. Jesus simplified this Old Testament covenant with the obligation to love God and our neighbor. Your marriage is a covenant relationship following in the great traditions of the Bible as God's Word revealed to all people. Your marriage reaffirmation does not suggest that you discard the past and start over but, like the new covenant in Christ's blood, that you seek to perfectly fulfill the covenant you made to each other on your wedding day. So today, you may renew that solemn promise verbally and symbolically before this community and commit your lives anew to Christ and to your holy marriage vows.

2. A family is a life form. There is a mystical union between family members, just as there is a mystical union between Christians through Christ. There is discord in families, just as there is discord in the Body of Christ. Yet there are binding forces that pull Christian families together under the most difficult of circumstances. The Christian faith offers unique powers and strengths to families of every description. The marriage ceremony is a worship service in which the triangular relationship between man, woman, and God is affirmed (Eccl. 4:9-12). Oneness through Christ is graciously offered by God as a gift to Christian marriages (Matt. 19:4-6).

3. Christians who marry make a special commitment to a love that is an act of will, as well as of emotion. With God's help it is possible to keep this commitment—to realize it as a source of freedom, in the same way commitment to God is freeing. The marriage relationship has a special capacity for spiritual and emotional growth, conveying the character of God's unconditional love—a love that sacrifices, forgives, sustains, and affirms (1 Cor. 13).

INVITATION TO MARRIAGE VOW RENEWAL:

Many pressures confront families and marriages today. In our worship we have responded to these pressures by affirming our families. In response to the pressures on marriage, I now invite you to remember and reaffirm your marriage vows. Reaffirmation of those vows is a sign that you will continue in your commitment to a growing relationship and openness to God. If this would be meaningful to you as a married couple, please come forward at this time.

(It is advisable to contact several couples before the service to explain the ceremony and ask if they would be among the first couples to come forward.)

REAFFIRMATION OF THE MARRIAGE VOWS:

The pastor shall say to the husband (husbands):

Will you continue in your commitment to have this woman as your wedded wife, to live together in the holy estate of matrimony? Will you continue to love her, comfort her, honor and keep her, in sickness and in health, and remain faithful to her so long as you both shall live?

The husband (husbands) shall answer, "I will."

Then the pastor shall say to the wife (wives):

Will you continue in your commitments to have this man as your wedded husband, to live together in the holy estate of matrimony? Will you continue to love him, comfort him, honor and keep him, in sickness and in health, and remain faithful to him so long as you both shall live?

The wife (wives) shall answer, "I will."

Then the pastor shall say:

Take the hands of your spouse now, and as confirmation that you will continue to uphold your marriage vows, repeat those vows once again. The husband (husbands) will repeat after me:

I (husband's name) take you (wife's name) . . . to be my wife . . . to have and to hold . . . from this day forward . . . for better, for worse . . . for richer, for poorer . . . in sickness and in health . . . to love and to cherish . . . till death us do part . . . according to God's holy ordinance . . . and thereto I pledge you my faith.

Then the pastor shall say:

The wife (wives) will repeat after me:

I (wife's name) take you (husband's name) . . . to be my wife . . . to have and to hold . . . from this day forward . . . for better, for worse . . . for richer, for poorer . . . in sickness and in health . . . to love and to cherish . . . till death us do part . . . according to God's holy ordinance . . . and thereto I pledge you my faith.

CLOSING PRAYER

BENEDICTION